The Batt

Brighton

1377

Leonard James

Acknowledgements

Photos, illustrations and maps are by the author except:
Tomb of Bertrand du Gueslcin, David.Monniaux; Jean de Vienne, Zaqarbal; Ypres
Tower, Tony Hisgett; Carisbrooke Castle, Mark Hogan; Hastings Castle, Kreepin Deth;
Brighton seafront, Bojan Lazarevic; Royal Pavilion, Purin Wangkiratikant; St
Nicholas's Church, Hassocks5489;

Website - www.BretwaldaBooks.com
Twitter - @Bretwaldabooks
Facebook - Bretwalda Books
Blog - bretwaldabooks.blogspot.co.uk/

Bretwalda Books
Unit 8, Fir Tree Close, Epsom,
Surrey KT17 3LD
info@BretwaldaBooks.com
www.BretwaldaBooks.com
ISBN 978-1-909698-88-8

CONTENTS

CHAPTER 1
THE 100 YEARS' WAR

By the time the French landed at Brighton to loot, kill and rape, the Hundred Years War was already 40 years old and had claimed tens of thousands of lives. The war would rage on for generations after Brighton, laying waste large areas of France, claiming vast numbers of lives and leaving a legacy of bitterness between the two nations that has never really gone away. The Battle fought just outside Brighton in June 1377 was one of the rare occasions when the war spilled over on to English soil, but it was nonetheless savage for that.

The Hundred Years War is usually treated by historians as a dynastic one between the royal houses of England and France. That is true so far as it goes, but lurking behind the dynastic claims were economic and trade disputes that embraced not only England and France, but also much of Europe. It was those wider disputes that brought the war to Brighton in the summer of 1377.

As the 13th century turned into the 14th the trade routes of Europe were undergoing dramatic strategic changes that were related to new forms of transport and to novel ways of doing business that remain familiar today. In the 1160s merchants in several towns around the Baltic established the Hanseatic League. The league worked to promote trade and to lower taxes and tariffs so that they could make more money for themselves. The key driver in the Hanseatic League was the cog, a new type of ship that could cope with the rough seas of the Baltic, North and Irish Seas while carrying larger amounts of cargo than earlier types of ship.

By the 1330s the Hanseatic League had expanded to include not only nearly every port around the Baltic, but also those around the North Sea and English Channel. The Hansa warehouses in London were along what is now Upper Thames Street just west of London Bridge in the heart of the City of London.

It was in the Low Countries that the extensive trade networks of the Hanseatic League met those of the Cloth Fairs that were held at cities and towns across France and parts of Germany. These attracted merchants from most of Western

The first pitched battle of the 100 Years War was the English naval victory at Sluys which gave the English control of the Channel for a generation. The English wool trade to the Low Countries could continue largely unaffected by the war.

and Southern Europe. By the 1320s merchant ships from as far afield as Italy were sailing direct to the Low Countries bringing huge cargoes of spices and silks from the East as well as other products from the Mediterranean.

All this trading was revolutionised in the Low Countries by innovative ways of doing business. In about the 1270 merchants in Bruges invented what we know today as the limited company. Instead of trading with their own money, and risking personal bankruptcy if things went wrong, they pooled some of their money into a trading venture that had a separate legal identity. This venture then made profits to be shared out, or losses to be bourne, by the merchants who had put money into the venture to start with. This exciting and flexible arrangement made it possible to take risks jointly, allowing merchants to embark on voyages, ventures and deals that no one man could ever have contemplated. In 1309 the Bourse was founded as a place where shares in these ventures could be bought and sold - effectively the world's first stock exchange. The world's first modern banks were also founded to fund the new mercantile activity. By 1320 Bruges and surrounding towns had become economic powerhouses.

All this happened under the control of successive Counts of Flanders who took a great interest in the new forms of business and sought to find ways to tax them without destroying them. In this the Counts of Flanders were highly unusual in

Europe. Most medieval monarchs drew their wealth from land and agriculture. They viewed merchants, particularly wealthy ones, as dreadful upstarts with money far above their social status and saw them only as targets to tax or plunder.

The Counts of Flanders had a vague and dangerously ambivalent status. They had been subjects of the Frankish Empire, but since the 11th century had owed a nominal allegiance to the Kings of France, while enjoying wide rights of self government. So long as Flanders was an impoverished swamp the Kings of France did not seek to exercise their nominal overlordship, but as Flanders grew rich the French kings regarded the region with greedy eyes.

The growing business boom in the Low Countries centred on the cloth trade, and particularly on wool. Raw wool was brought into the Low Countries, processed into a wide variety of cloths of different colours and finishes, then exported again. The main sources of wool were England and Spain, while the markets for cloth embraced most of Western Europe.

The fact that by the 1320s most of England's foreign trade was in the form of wool to Flanders made the Kings of England view events in Flanders with great interest. The increasing friction between the Count of Flanders and his overlord, the King of France, thus became of importance to the Kings of England.

They were also of dynastic interest. The men who were Kings of England were also Dukes of Aquitaine and Dukes of Gascony. All of these lands, and others, were part of the Kingdom of France. This meant that the King of England, as Duke of Aquitaine, was a subject of the King of France just as was the Count of Flanders. Efforts by the King of France to impose his rule and taxes on the Count of Flanders was thus of real interest to the King of England since his lands in Aquitaine, and elsewhere, might be the next to feel the sting of French taxes and rules. To complicate matters still further the Kings of England were descended from the Dukes of Normandy and Counts of Anjou and still had claims to those regions of France, although the French kings did not recognise those claims. Such defunct claims could, however, be useful bargaining chips and cropped up in the increasingly fraught diplomatic moves between France and England.

This was the complicated and rather ill-tempered state of relations between England and France in 1328 when King Charles IV of France died leaving only daughters as his children. The Salic Law of the Kingdom of France forbade a woman to rule, so there followed a two month pause while the French nobles tried to decide who would be the next King of France.

None of the three men with the strongest claims the French throne had a claim that was obviously stronger than the others. Philip of Burgundy was the son of Joan, the daughter of the previous French king Philip V. His claim was quickly discarded on the grounds that he was only five years old. That meant that he would be in the hands of a regent and council for some years, and since his father Duke Odo of Burgundy was a quarrelsome man with ongoing disputes with several French nobles, nobody wanted him as regent.

The second claimant was King Edward III of England, who was the son of Charles IV's sister Isabella which made him the nephew of the dead king. The French nobles weren't too keen on having Edward as their king. This was partly because he was powerful in his own right, and so would be difficult to push around, and partly because they feared he would use his position as King of France to grab back all the titles and lands that his ancestors had lost - and in so doing deprive the French nobles of valuable estates. Edward did not push his claim as he was engaged in putting down a rebellion by Roger Mortimer, Earl of March, and knew that very soon he would face a war with Scotland.

The third claimant was Philip, Count of Valois. He was the son of Count Charles of Valois who was himself the son of King Philip III of France, who had died in 1285. From the pont of view of the French nobles Philip of Valois was the best bet. He was French, he was a noble who shared their concerns and views, and he was relatively poor and weak so he was unlikely to be a strong ruler who would keep the nobles in their place.

Having decided on Philip of Valois as the next king, the French nobles had to

King Edward III of England in a 19th century engraving. The two crowns on his sword symbolise his rule of England and his claim to be King of France. Although historians often treat the 100 Years' War as one fought for purely dynastic reasons, there were economic disputes and rivalries that underpinned much of the trouble between England and France in the 14th Century.

7

A cog, the type of ship used most widely in northern waters during the 14th Century. The ship was primarily a merchant vessel which had a large hold to carry cargo and needed only a relatively small crew to operate. In times of war these ships were fitted with temporary platforms at bow and stern, as here, from which armed men could gain the advantage of height over those on the decks of enemy ships.

find some way to justify their choice. They turned to a group of lawyers and churchmen in Paris, who duly obliged. They declared that the Salic Law not only forbade a woman to rule France, but it also forbade a woman to transmit the right to rule to her son. This was an entirely novel interpretation of the law that nobody had ever heard of before, but it suited the French nobles so they accepted it. This new ruling excluded both Philip of Burgundy and Edward of England, and so Philip of Valois became King Philip VI of France.

In May 1337 Philip VI met with his Grand Council in Paris. They decided that the Duchy of Aquitaine should be confiscated from King Edward III of England because Edward was allowing the fugitive Robert of Artois to live in England. Edward countered that he was using his role as King of England to allow Robert of Artois to live in England, and that if Robert ever went to Aquitaine he would, of course, be handed over to Philip VI. Philip hit back accusing Edward of "other transgressions", which he never identified, and announced that Aquitaine and Gascony were both confiscated. Edward reacted by stating that Philip had no right to confiscate the two duchies since he was not the rightful King of France anyway, that honour belonging to himself. King Edward III of England announced that he was really King Edward I of France and called on the nobles of France to dethrone Philip and recognise Edward as their true monarch.

Only a few French nobles sided with Edward, but it gave Edward the legal right to hold on to his possessions in France. War was, of course, inevitable. It began in the Low Countries where several minor lords and towns recognised Edward. After some years of desultory siege operations and diplomatic moves to gain allies, the war erupted in 1346 with a major English invasion of northern France that culminated in the Battle of Crecy in 1346. Philip VI died in 1350, to

A Victorian view of the Black Prince leading the English advance at the Battle of Crecy in 1346. The battle was a stunning victory for a small English army over a much larger French force. Although this picture gives the credit to Prince Edward, the Black Prince, eldest son of King Edward III, the victory was in fact more due to the massed volleys of arrows shot by English archers and by incompetence on the part of the French commanders than it was to the young, dashing prince.

be replaced by his son John II. The French navy had already been almost annihilated at the Battle of Sluys in 1240, so Edward was free to move armies where he liked. He next invaded France through Aquitaine, winning another great victory at Poitier in 1356 at which he captured King John II of France.

More campaigns followed in which the English won impressive victories and conquered wide territories, but were never quite able to entirely defeat the French. In 1366 civil war broke out in the Kingdom of Castile, the largest and richest of the kingdoms in Spain, between Pedro and his brother Henry, both of whom claimed to be the true king. King Charles VII, the new King of France, sent an army to support Henry. Edward of England did not want a French ally on the southern border of Aquitaine, so he sent an army to back Pedro. In 1369 Pedro was killed in battle and Henry became the King of Castile with a thoroughly hostile attitude to England.

In 1371 Edward III became ill, as did his eldest son and heir Edward the Black Prince. That led to a lack of campaigning energy in France and allowed the French to regain lost ground. The weakness of Edward III's grip on power was demonstrated in 1376 by a legal action brought against Alice Perrers, Edward's mistress and mother of his three illegitimate children. The action alleged that Perrers had gained possession of a manor through corruption and although she ultimately won the case it would never have been brought in public against the king's mistress a few years earlier.

Much of the French success was due to the inspired leadership of a Breton nobleman Bertrand du Guesclin who was appointed Constable of France, effectively Commander in Chief of the French military. Learning of the breakdown in royal authority in England, du Guesclin sensed an opportunity. The French navy had never recovered from its appalling defeat at Sluys, but King Henry of Castile had a good navy and du Guesclin had a good army.

It was time to invade England.

The bust from the tomb of Bertrand du Guesclin at St Denis Basilica, near Paris. It was du Guesclin who brought the French back from the brink of defeat in the first part of the 100 Years' War and who conceived the strategy of invading England.

Chapter 2
Commanders at Brighton

The guiding hand behind the campaign that brought war to Brighton and the surrounding area was that of the French supreme commander, Bertrand du Guesclin. It was his idea to invade England and his organisational skills that put together both the fleet and the army that came to Sussex in June 1377.

Du Guesclin was born in about 1320 near Dinan in Brittany to Robert du Guesclin, a minor noble whose wealth was barely greater than that of a rural knight. In 1341 he rallied to Charles of Blois during the Breton civil war that broke out in 1341. After a series of successful actions and a long guerilla campaign du Guesclin ended up on the winning side. He was then retained by King Charles V of France to help in the war against England.

His campaign against the English began with a crushing victory over the English ally King Charles II of Navarre (a kingdom in the Pyrenees that is now divided between France and Spain) in 1364. His next task was to lead an army composed almost entirely of mercenaries into Spain to help the French protege Henry of Trastamara in the civil war raging in Castile. It was du Guesclin who caused the death of Henry's rival Pedro and thus decided that civil war in favour of France's interests.

In 1370 du Guesclin returned to France where he was made Constable of France, the highest military rank in the kingdom. He promptly defeated an English army at the Battle of Pontvallain, then carefully manoeuvred his way around the English supply lines to force their larger army led by the Black Prince out of Poitou and Saintonge. Realising that the English were feeding constant supplies of men and equipment into Bordeaux by sea, du Guesclin called on King Henry of Castile to send the Castilian fleet to cut the sea lanes. In June 1372 the Castilian fleet, led by the Genoese admiral Ambrosio Boccanegra ambushed an English supply fleet off La Rochelle. Of the 57 English ships, 48 were sunk or captured while the Castilians lost no ships at all and had only a few dozen men killed.

Now free of the continual English superiority in terms of men and munitions, du Guesclin began the process of conquering Aquitaine and Gascony. By the spring of 1374 that campaign was still dragging on, but du Guesclin was starting to look elsewhere for opportunities to hurt the English. He knew that since the Battle of Sluys the English ships had ruled the English Channel unopposed. Du Guesclin reasoned that this might mean that the coastal defences had been neglected. It is not known if he questioned merchants who visited England, but the way the naval campaigns developed over the following years it seems very likely that he did. At any rate he had good intelligence from somewhere.

Again du Guesclin asked for naval help from King Henry of Castile, and again the Spaniard responded. This time the Castilian fleet was commanded by a native Castilian, Fernando Sánchez de Tovar. Tovar was in his thirties, though his precise age is unknown. He had started his life as a soldier and had fought in several actions during the Castilian civil war that put Henry on the throne. When Ambrosio Boccanegra died in 1373 Henry chose the loyal and reliable Tovar to succeed him.

Although he was a landsman, Tovar took his new job seriously and lost no time in going to sea. He immersed himself in maritime lore, talked endlessly to sailors and captains and within a couple of years had become an accomplished admiral. In the spring of 1374 the Castilian ships came north, entered the English Channel and landed a force on the Isle of Wight. The Spanish spent three days roaming at

The French admiral Jean de Vienne had begun his military career as a knight fighting on land in conventional fashion. It was only after he was made commander in chief of all French naval forces in the Atlantic and Channel that he began learning about how naval warfare was conducted. He learned fast, quickly grasping the opportunities that fast-moving ships gave him when attacking the southern coast of England. It was Vienne who led the French army that landed at Brighton in the summer of 1377.

12

will across the island looting everything they could find and burning every village in sight. They withdrew without capturing Carisbrooke Castle, the main stronghold of the island, but even so the daring raid had been a blow to English morale and prestige. Tova stopped off in France to hold talks with the newly appointed French admiral Jean de Vienne, then went home.

In 1375 Tovar and his ships were back. This time Tovar failed to find any weakly protected targets and he was heading home before the autumn storms began when on 10 August 1375 he was cruising south off the Breton coast and passed the Bay of Bourgneuf. Sheltering in the bay Tovar saw a large fleet of English merchant ships, which he promptly attacked. The English ships scattered and fled, but even so Tovar managed to capture 39 ships.

Tovar sailed home loudly declaring that he had won what he called the "Battle of Bourgneuf", but he was soon in trouble. The kings of France, Castile and England had agreed a truce some weeks earlier that had begun on 2 August. It was for this reason that the English merchant ships had felt it safe to put into a French port to take on fresh cargo and why they had not fled fast enough when Tovar approached. When news of the disaster reached England the merchants who had lost ships put in a combined claim for compensation of £18,000. Edward III passed the bill on to Henry of Castile and the diplomatic wrangling went on for years before a sum was finally agreed and paid.

The year 1376 passed quietly for Tovar since the truce between the three belligerent kingdoms lasted until 1 April 1377. But Tovar did not waste his time, he spent much of it liaising with Vienne about how to attack England the next year.

Like Tovar, Vienne was given command of the French navy due to his valour as a knight and proven loyalty to the French crown rather than his skills as a naval man. Also like Tovar, however, Vienne threw himself enthusiastically into his new job as "Amiral de France" when he was given the job in 1373 at the age of 32. Vienne had been born at Dole to a relatively obscure knightly family and at the age of 19 went to war as an esquire in the retinue of a local nobleman. He was knight at 21 and soon had his own independent commands patrolling border areas and probing for weaknesses in English-held territory. The decision of the king to make him an admiral seems to have come as a surprise, but he was soon hard at work.

At first Vienne saw his role as a defensive one. He organised a series of mounted patrols on land to keep a watch for English landings and ordered the construction of a large number of small, fast ships to patrol the coastal waters, again to watch for English moves and ships. Soon, possibly under the influence of Tovar, Vienne was thinking about a more aggressive role for the French navy. He began an aggressive lobbying drive to get more money from the French government, and began building ships designed and equipped for war.

By the spring of 1377, Vienne still had much less naval experience than did Tovar, but he was learning fast. He had spent a lot of time at sea, and had a wealth of fighting experience on land. He was a seasoned and capable commander.

In overall charge of the English anti-invasion preparations in the southern counties was Sir Robert Hales, the Grand Prior of the Knights Hospitallar in England. It might sound odd to modern ears for the leader of an organisation dedicated to fighting the Moslem hordes on Crusade to be found leading one Christian army against another, but in medieval times senior clerics were frequently seconded from their official duties to undertake tasks for their monarch.

Hales had been born in about 1325 in High Halden, Kent, where his father Sir

The arms of Edmund of Langley, Earl of Cambridge, whose decision to go to London to join the political feuding at court rather than stay at his post at Dover Castle contributed to French success in 1377. As the son of a monarch, Cambridge was entitled to carry the royal coat of arms, though it had to be distinguished by a three-pronged white band called a "label argent" which because he was the fourth son carried three red balls.

14

Nicholas Hales was a moderately prosperous landowner and knight. As a younger son, Hales would not inherit the family lands so he joined the Knights Hospitallar as a career. He went to the Holy Land more than once and in 1365 he joined an invasion of Egypt led by King Peter I of Cyprus. He was back in England by 1370 and two years later became head of the Hospitalars in England. He had a reputation for bravery in battle and generosity to his fellows, though some considered him to be aloof and proud.

The English forces were raised at short notice and were unavoidably less well organised than those of the invaders. It is not entirely certain who was in command of the English army though most contemporaries state that it was John de Caroloco, Prior of Lewes.

Caroloco was a Frenchman who had moved to England to take up his position as prior in 1366. He is thought to have been aged about 40. As Prior of Lewes he held no official position in the military hierarchy of Sussex. However, the majority of the lands in the area were owned by Lewes Priory, so it is reasonable to assume that most of the militia men who mustered in Lewes to defend the area came from priory lands. It was usual for men to be commanded by their lord or a leading local landowner so while having a churchman in this role was unusual, it was not unheard of. Presumably Caroloco appointed himself commander on the grounds that he had brought more men to the muster than anyone else. Certainly he intended to play an active role in any fighting that was to take place for he wore a suit of armour, over which was a cloak of red velvet. So far as is known he had absolutely no military experience or training at all.

The next most senior Englishman on the field of battle was Sir Thomas Cheyne, a grizzled veteran of the French Wars who was aged about 60 years old. Cheyne had been closely associated with the Black Prince for several years and may have been one of his retainers, though this is uncertain. What is known is that Cheyne took part in numerous campaigns in France and that he fought at the great victory of Najera in 1367 when the Black Prince defeated du Guesclin. As a young man Cheyne had won himself a handsome fortune by capturing senior French knights and holding them to ransom - then an honourable part of warfare. He invested his money in that traditional aristocratic moneyspinner rich agricultural land and by 1377 was comfortably ensconced at his manor at Farnborough in Surrey.

Given his advancing years and the recent death of his patron, Cheyne may have considered himself due a bit of rest and a break from the fighting. It was not to be. He had known the Earl of Arundel well during his service with the Black

Prince so Cheyne responded when Arundel summoned men to help him defend Sussex. Cheyne seems to have been serving for cash payment and was probably stationed in Lewes Castle where his many years as a soldier would have put him in the ideal position to give advice to the local men.

Another of Arundel's hired lances was Sir John Falvesley from Northamptonshire, who was around 40 years old. Falvesley had been a retainer of Lionel, Duke of Clarence, another son of Edward III. Wie know that Falvesley accompanied Clarence on a number of long journeys, including to Ireland in 1365 but his longest journey was to Italy. Clarence made the journey to marry the beautiful Violante, daughter of the staggeringly wealthy but notoriously cruel and ruthless Galleazzo Visconti, Lord of Padua and ruler of Milan. The journey to Milan through Germany was a long procession of parties and receptions, followed by a lavish wedding in Milan itself in June 1368. Visconti handed over an enormous dowry of 200,000 gold florins, but he grabbed it straight back when Clarence died only a few weeks later of a sudden fever. There were rumours at the time that Visconti had turned against Clarence for some reason and had him murdered.

The sudden death had left Falvesley stranded in Italy. He joined a band of mercenaries fighting for the Papacy, gaining experience of how wars were fought in Italy. He was back in England by 1372 and the

This man's equipment is the ideal to which the English militia infantry would aspire, though many would fail to have the full kit. His helmet is of iron, padded inside with a thick leather lining stuffed with wool. The mail hauberk has a coif under the helmet and reaches to the thighs and elbows. Over the hauberk he wears a sleeveless tunic made of thick leather on to which have been sewn overlapping scales made from horn. His triangular shield is about 30 inches tall and 24 inches wide and is made of thin, overlapping sheets of wood faced with boiled leather. His main weapon is a 10 foot long thrusting spear, with a short sword for back up.

following year he joined John of Gaunt on a spectacularly impressive campaign in France that saw the English army march all the way from Calais to Bordeaux, fighting dozens of battles along the way.

There can be no doubt that Falvesley was the most experienced of the knights with the English army, though he was apparently considered to be junior to both Caroloco and Cheyne.

Also present was an esquire named John Brocas, who had come to England from Gascony as a child. He was aged about 25 in 1377 and had yet to achieve

William de Montacute, the Earl of Salisbury, was English commander of defences in the counties of Dorset and Wiltshire in 1377. With no French invaders in his own territory, but hearing of the landings in Kent and Sussex, Salisbury decided to march a force east to help bolster defences where the French were landing in numbers. He arrived a few hours too late to take part in the Battle of Brighton.

his knighthood. He held lands near Shopwyke, just outside Chichester, and at Exceat. Although only an esquire the land he held obliged to him serve the Earl of Arundel as a knight in terms of equipment and tactical deployment. His father and grandfather had both served alongside the Black Prince, but Brocas himself does not seem to have been on campaign.

Every contemporary source of the battle mentions the fact that Thomas Wilford was present, so it must be assumed that he was important at the time. All we know about Wilford is that he was the parson of Ardingley, but that he rarely visited his parish and left the care of his flock to a curate. Instead Wilford worked as a clerk at Westminster in the Chancery where his neat handwriting made him useful copying out duplicates of government charters, patents and letters. Presumably he was with the gathering local militia in Lewes to ensure that the paperwork was all kept in order, though it is less easy to understand either why he went to fight with the army or why he was considered important enough to be mentioned when so many others of similar status were not.

Although he arrived too late to play a major role in the battle, mention should be made of William de Montacute, Earl of Salisbury. He was by far the most senior of the English commanders involved in the struggle around Brighton as he not only held the rank of earl, but also came from an old and high ranking family. He was aged 51 and had fought alongside the Black Prince at the Battle of Poitiers in 1356 and had taken part in numerous other campaigns in France as well as serving as a diplomat on behalf of Edward III to agree truces.

As a young man Salisbury had got himself involved in a tangled sexual scandal - though the fault was not his. In 1341 he married Joan, daughter of the Earl of Kent, whose astonishing beauty and charm earned her the nickname of "The Fair Maid of Kent". In 1355, however, a knight named Sir Thomas Holland came back to England after years away on Crusade. Holland had been a poor man when he left, but now came back rich. Joan now announced that she had been secretly married to Holland before he went abroad, a claim backed up by both Holland and the priest who had married them. For a young noble lady to marry a penniless knight without her parent's permission was scandalous enough, but for her then to bigamously marry an earl was astonishing for the time and the scandal was the talk of all Europe. Given the social status of the parties involved the Pope himself was called in to sort out the mess. He decided that Joan was really married to Holland, and so Salisbury lost his wife. Salisbury married again, but a final twist to the story came when Holland died and Joan promptly married the Black Prince.

She thus became the wife of Salisbury's greatest friend and mother of the future King Richard II.

In spring 1377 Salisbury had been put in charge of the defences of Dorset and Wiltshire. He had mustered his retainers and put the local militia on alert. His detailed actions and movements have not been recorded, but at some point after hearing of the burning of Rye, Salisbury decided to march to Kent. He must have thought that the local commanders were making a mess of things and needed his help. He and his army were marching east along the northern edge of the South Downs. We do not know exactly where Salisbury's army was when the French landed at Brighton, but it is certain that the militia gathering in Lewes did not know that they were in the area, so presumably they had not yet arrived and must have been several miles to the west.

This cavalry man would have been called a hobilar in 1377 and was typical of the horsemen raised by the English militia. He wears an iron helmet with mail hanging down to protect his neck and shoulders. His body armour is composed of quilted linen up to 18 layers thick, which was surprisingly effective, reaching to his knees. His main weapon is a lance, but he also carries a sword and a dagger. Hobilars were used to scout ahead of an army and to ride ahead to find camping grounds, search for food supplies or locate the enemy. At Brighton they seem to have been present in only small numbers and played only a limited role in the fighting.

Chapter 3
The Campaign before Brighton

Everyone had known for months that the truce between England and France would end on 1 April 1377, and both sides should have been getting ready to renew the fighting. In the event it was the French who moved first. The French admiral Jean de Vienne had long been discussing plans for the summer of 1377 with his Castilian opposite number Fernando Sánchez de Tovar. They had decided that the Castilian fleet would come north as soon as the spring weather allowed, whereupon the combined fleets would launch a series of hit and run raids on the South Coast of England to probe defences, and perhaps organise a proper invasion if circumstances allowed.

News of this arrangement leaked out and in January 1377 the Bishop of St David's, Chancellor of England, announced the news to the English Parliament. Authority was given to spend money hiring crews and commandeering ships of over 20 tons. The ships were to gather in the Thames at the end of March, while a large army was to muster in Kent. Instructions were sent to the mayors of coastal towns and the Sheriffs of coastal counties to be ready to muster their men for instant action in the event of a French landing.

As commander of the defence of the kingdom in the south, Sir Robert Hales, went to work. He was, however, hindered by the gathering political crisis caused by the declining health of the aging King Edward III. The heir to the throne was the ten year old Richard, son of Edward's eldest son who had died in 1376. However, Edward's younger son John of Gaunt, Duke of Lancaster, was ambitious, rich and powerful. He took it as read that he would be regent for the boy king, but many other noblemen worried that he would try to grab the throne for himself and so sought to thwart his bid for the regency. The intense political manoeuvring meant that few politicians had time to think much about the English navy, and fewer still could be bothered to do anything much about it.

The crisis suddenly got worse in May when King Edward III had a relapse of a serious abscess that had caused him great pain the previous year and which had removed him from government. Just a few days later word came from Flanders that the Castilian fleet had arrived at the port of Harfleur in the mouth of the Seine to rendezvous with the French fleet. An alarm was sent out to all the southern counties instructing them to get ready for a French landing. Rumours were rife that King Charles V of France planned a massive invasion and was intent on capturing London, and with it the ailing king. Edward was moved upriver to Sheen Manor, the nearest royal residence to London.

The Ypres Tower at Rye was built to be the key point of the town's defences in 1249 and in 1377 had been recently updated and modernised. However, severe damage to other parts of the town's defences by recent floods meant that the town was abandoned as soon as the French appeared.

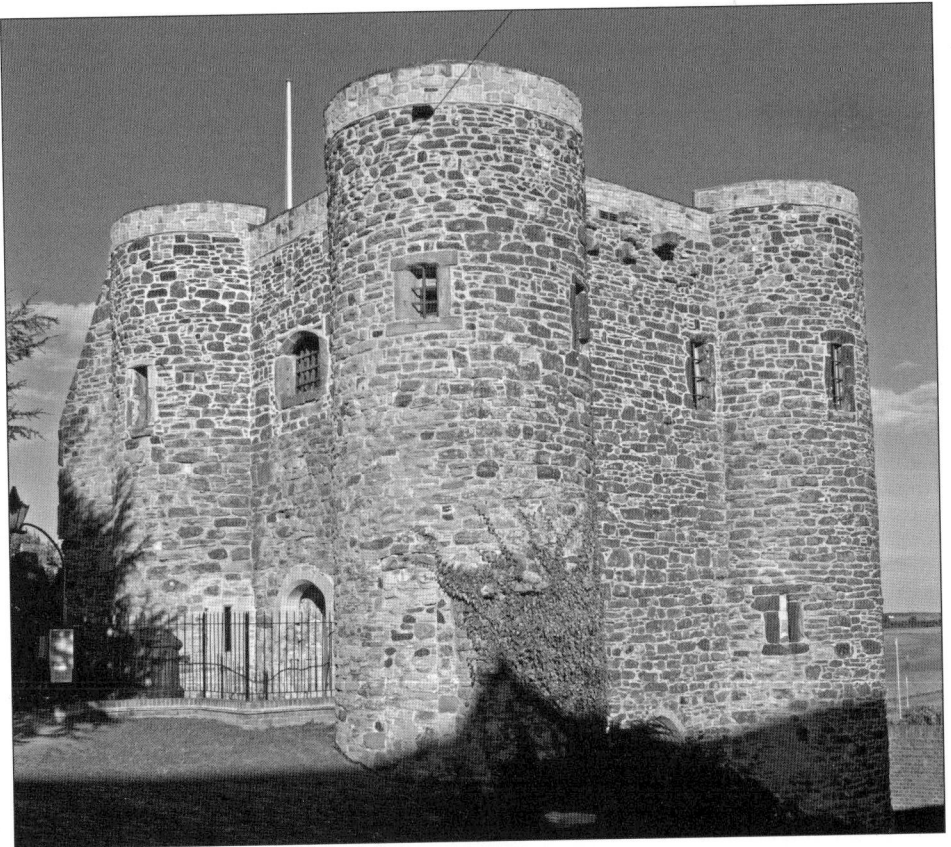

One of Edward's actions at Sheen was to appoint the Earl of Cambridge to be Constable of Dover Castle and Warden of the Cinque Ports - effectively putting him in charge of defences from London to Portsmouth under Hales's overall command of the southern shires. Edmund, Earl of Cambridge, was aged 36 and was Edward's fourth son. He had fought extensively in France through the 1360s and in 1375 had led a fleet to relieve the English garrison besieged in Brest.

On 21 June King Edward III died. His grandson was swiftly hailed as King Richard II and a Council of Nobles was appointed to advise him on the running of the kingdom. This neatly got around the question of who should be regent since none was appointed, but instead disputes about who should be on the Council intensified. Another source of intrigue was the conduct of the coronation, with assorted nobles vying for the prestigious roles for themselves and best seats for their wives and daughters.

The Earl of Cambridge almost immediately abandoned his post in Dover and returned to London to join the jostling for position among the senior nobles. He left in charge of his defensive duties three junior noblemen: Lord Latimer, Lord Cobham and Lord Clinton. Of these three, Clinton and Cobham were landowners in Kent who had no known military background, but did have the wealth and social contacts to get some sort of defence organised in the county.

William, Baron Latimer, was a more important and controversial figure. Aged about 50, he had fought at the Battle of Crecy in 1346 and had campaigned tirelessly throughout much of the 1350s and 1360s in France, successfully leading a number of minor campaigns and sieges. It came as something of a shock when he was arrested in 1376 on charges of corruption. He was found guilty of taking cash from French merchants to release their ships after they were captured, of withholding taxes he had collected but had not passed on to the government and of defrauding the king by producing fake documents "proving" non-existent loans made to the king in France and then demanding repayment. He was fined and thrown into prison. However, Latimer was a well known crony of John of Gaunt, who persuaded his father, Edward III to pardon the miscreant.

Latimer's appointment to help Cambridge was his first government job after his disgrace. Despite his crimes it must have been hoped that his undoubted military skill and talent would be useful in defending the realm. It was probably Latimer who organised the chain of beacons that spread across the southern counties. Every parish was to have a large bonfire located at a central spot. Scouts were positioned next to beacons located on the coast. If they saw an enemy fleet

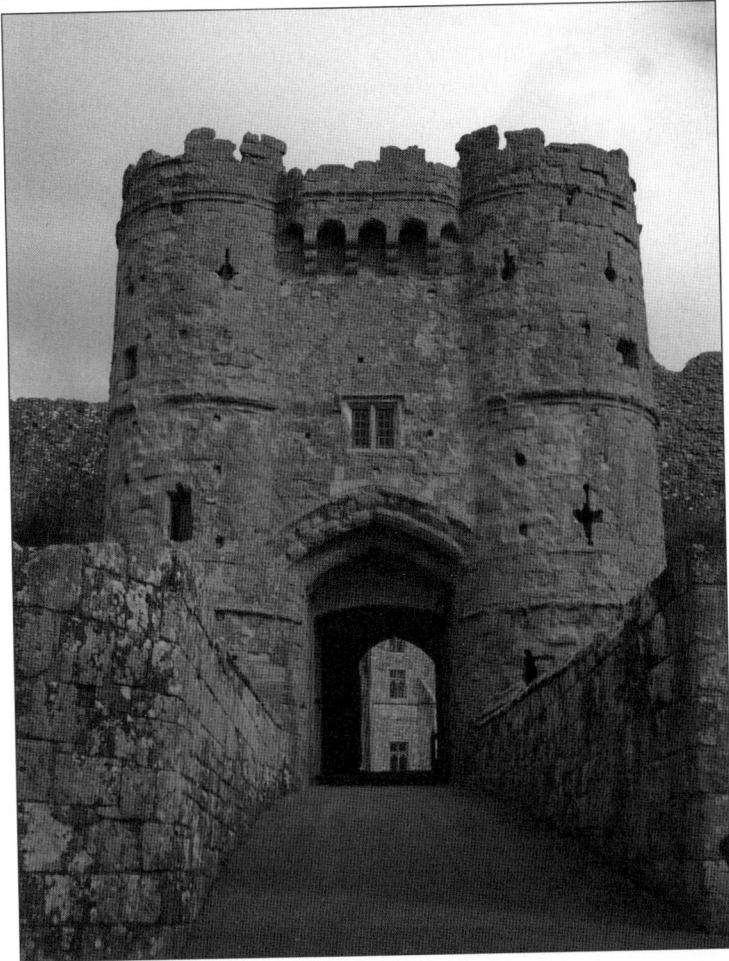

Carisbrooke Castle on the Isle of Wight managed to hold out against the French raiders, but the rest of the island was pillaged and the local authorities were persuaded at swordpoint to pay the raiders a large sum of cash to go away without burning every building to the ground.

approaching they were to set fire to their beacon. Those manning nearby beacons who saw the smoke by day or flames by night were to light their own beacon. Any man who saw a beacon was to grab whatever weapons he had to hand and assemble at the beacon to await orders.

The first beacon to flare into life was lit on the morning of 6 July and was that at Romney, overlooking the open waterway that then swept inland over what is now Romney Marsh to the estuaries of the rivers Rother and Brede. Other beacons took up the alarm and soon right across the counties of Kent and Sussex beacons

A mounted knight wearing what would have been the very latest armour in the 1370s, making this man most likely to be a nobleman. His helmet is shaped from a single sheet of steel hammered into a curved shape that would deflect incoming blows. The visor hinges upward to allow the man to breathe and see more easily when not in action. His chest, back, arms and upper legs are covered by plate armour, similarly shaped from sheets of steel. Mail protects his hands, feet and neck areas where flexibility is more important. His main weapon is the broadsword that hangs from his belt, though he would have had a short sword or axe as back up. His shield would have carried his own coat of arms, if he was entitled to one, or that of his patron if not.

were throwing up their columns of smoke and men were grabbing weapons and marching to their mustering points.

The total strength of the Franco-Castilian fleet was 120 ships, including 35 large ones owned by the King of France, and eight Castilian galleys commanded by Tovar. On board were four to five thousand troops, plus sailors and oarsmen. However, we know that Vienne kept some ships at sea and that others were patrolling the South Coast on the look out for any English warships coming to give battle. Quite how many ships and men took part in the attack on Rye is unclear.

The enemy fleet swept past and headed northwest toward the important port of Rye. The town is now more than two miles inland, but in 1377 it stood on a headland jutting out into the shallow waters of the Romney inlet, which surrounded it on three sides. Although it was an important port, Rye was in a bad condition. In 1375 a huge flood had swept away the eastern docks, dozens of houses and a long section of town wall. The damage was considered to be irreparable so the western docks (today the Strand) were improved and work was begun on building a new section of town wall along what is now New Road.

However, the new town wall was incomplete in 1377 and Rye was effectively defenceless. As soon as the smoke from the beacon went up those citizens still in the town made a run for it. Everything of value was either buried, hidden or loaded on to a cart that was whipped rapidly along the Hawkhurst Road, now the A268.

The main defence of Rye at this date was the Ypres Tower, a state of the art castle with rounded towers and high walls. However the Ypres Tower was small and without the town walls to support it was unlikely to hold out for long. The garrison stayed long enough to ensure that the majority of the population was on its way, then filed out to form a rearguard to the straggling column of refugees heading north.

The Franco-Castilian force landed, led by a knight named Sir Jean de Raix. They stormed through the broken walls only to find the town abandoned. For several hours the men ransacked every house they could find, smashing down locked doors and forcing windows to gain access. Once Raix was certain that his men had stolen everything worth having, he gave the order to fire the town, which his men put into pratice with enthusiasm. Destroying a town by fire could be a surprisingly difficult task. Unless the place was tinder dry after a prolonged drought it was unlikely that flames would spread from one side of a street to another, or even from one house to the next. Each house had to be set alight individually, using furniture smashed for the purpose and piled up against an internal wooden wall or partition. Even St Mary's Church at the centre of the town was put to the torch, though its solid stone construction caused the damage to be limited.

Raix and his men then filed back to the ships, which cast off and sailed back across the Romney inlet to put out to sea. Behind them they left a huge column of smoke that reached high into the sky and could be seen for many miles about. The refugees strung out on the road to the north knew what it meant. And when word of the attack reached London the Royal Court knew what it meant as well.

"We must make haste to crown our king," declared one courtier. "And then we must go against the French, else they will do us great injury."

The coronation was hurriedly arranged for 16th July, for in medieval eyes a king was not truly a king until he had been blessed by the holy oils of God. The City of London was lavishly decorated by its citizens and the fountains ran with

The main gate into the town of Winchelsea. It was here that negotiations between the French invaders and the defenders were conducted. The defenders joked at the French expense, provoking the invaders into a furious assault that came close to success.

wine, not water, for the day. Even so there was no hiding the fact that it had all been done in a rush.

If the quick coronation was designed to frighten off Tovar and Viennes, it failed. Two days later the Franco-Castilian fleet sailed up the Solent and dropped anchor off Southampton. Commanding the garrison in Southampton was Sir John Arundel, younger brother of William Earl of Arundel. Arundel paraded his men along the town walls, then rode out of the town gates on to the dock side. Gorgeously turned out in his full armour and riding his great war horse, attended by his herald and his standard bearer, Arundel shouted defiance across the waters at the invaders.

For several hours Tovar and Viennes studied the defences of Southampton and counted the men that Arundel had paraded on the walls. Then, as the tide began to ebb, they lifted their anchors, unfurled their sails and sailed back down the Solent and out into the English Channel.

They did not go far and next day landed on the Isle of Wight. Tovar had, of course, been here before and knew the lie of the land. He knew that the key to the island was Carisbrooke Castle, and sent a fast-marching column of men to capture the place. The column of men was led by a French knight, possibly the Sir Jean de Raix who had led the landing at Rye. A second column went to Yarmouth and a third to Newtown, then the two biggest towns on the island.

The column that reached Carisbrooke found the gates of the castle firmly shut and the commander, Sir Hugh Tyrrel refusing even to discuss terms. The other columns encountered less opposition. Rather than spend time plundering and trying to find hidden treasures, Vienne offered the terrified civilians - who unlike those at Rye had nowhere to run - a deal. If they paid him 1,000 marks he would go away and leave both them and their property intact. A mark was the equivalent of 160 pennies, so at a time when the average workman was paid two pennies a day this was a huge sum of money. Nevertheless the people of the Isle of Wight managed to find the ready cash and handed it over.

Instead of leaving, however, Viennes merely settled down to lay siege to Carisbrooke Castle. A siege could be a tedious business, and Vienne had many demands on his time. Not least he had to use his ships to keep control of the Solent to stop any English relief force crossing over.

On a day when Viennes was absent and another French knight was in charge of the siege, Tyrell decided that the time had come to teach the French a lesson. Keeping his preparations hidden from French view, Tyrell mustered his men for a sally. First local knight Sir Peter de Heyno, who lived at Stenbury, offered to shoot the French commander. He fetched what he called his "silver bow" and stood at an arrowslit until the French knight came within sight. Pulling his bow back to its maximum bend, Heyno let loose. His arrow flew true, struck the French man in the chest and knocked him from his horse.

That was the signal Tyrell had been waiting for. The castle gates were thrown open and the English soldiers streamed out. A short, but savage battle followed that saw the besieging French overwhelmed by the sudden onslaught. Tyrell had brought lit torches and kindling with him, so he was quickly able to set fire to the French siege engines and made sure that they were well alight before pulling his men back into the castle.

The ruins of Hastings Castle with the town behind. For some unknown reason neither nor the town nor the castle were defended in 1377 so the small force of Frenchmen who came ashore here were free to loot the place without opposition, then set fire to the town and burn it to the ground.

When he heard of the sally, Viennes realised that he was not going to gain much more from the Isle of Wight. Calling Tyrell "a dangerous serpent", he abandoned the siege and marched his men back on board the ships. It was now 21 August.

While Viennes was busy on the Isle of Wight, the English had been taking additional steps to defend their shores. On 25 July an edict was issued in the name of Richard II ordering all churchmen to turn out their tenants and other men to join the militia. The ecclesiastics should have already done this since they were landholders like all others, so the fact that they had to be reminded by a special message would indicate that they had been dragging their feet. The Bishop of Chichester is known to have called out his men on 4 August, so it seems to have had the desired effect.

The Franco-Castilian fleet was next heard off at Winchelsea, though the date they appeared is not known. Like Rye, Winchelsea is now some distance from the sea, but in 1377 it too stood on a headland that was mostly surrounded by water and sheltered a port. The merchants of Winchelsea specialised in the Gascon wine trade and so had a direct interest in England retaining its control of that corner of France.

Unlike Rye, the town walls of Winchelsea were intact and neither the garrison nor townsfolk had any intention of leaving. The garrison had recently been greatly strengthened by the local militia who had Winchelsea as their mustering point. It was the Abbot of Battle Abbey who, by virtue of the large estates the abbey held in the area, was responsible for mustering the men of the area for war. It was therefore this abbot, Harno de Offynton, who appeared on the battlements of the gates of Winchelsea when Vienne marched up to the gates alongside his herald to open negotiations.

Vienne started by offering Winchelsea the same terms he had given the civilians on the Isle of Wight - pay a huge sum of cash in order to avoid having their houses and properties destroyed. Abbot Harno smiled down at Vienne and said that he was unwilling to buy back something that he had not lost. The Englishmen lining the walls laughed at their commander's jest, but Vienne smiled pleasantly enough.

Vienne's next proposal was that both sides should send out an equal number of men to fight in a field, the result of the combat deciding the fate of the town. If the Frenchmen won, Abbot Harno would pay up, but if the Englishmen won then Vienne would sail away. "I am a man of the Church," replied Harno, "so I cannot accept such a proposal. I did not come here for the purposes of war but for the preservation of peace among my flock." Having got nowhere in talks, but having observed the niceties of medieval warfare, Vienne withdrew to prepare his attack.

The French assault began at noon. Although we have no detailed record of the attack, it seems unlikely that Vienne had any heavy siege equipment with him. More likely he had scaling ladders. An assault of this kind would normally involve crossbowmen deluging the battlements with bolts to kill any unwary defenders and force the others to keep their heads down.

Once the section of wall to be attacked was clear of defenders, men would rush forwards with scaling ladders. The ladders would be put against the walls and the attackers clamber up. The crossbow bolts would continue to hit the wall parapet until the men climbing the ladders were almost at the top. There then followed a race between those on ladders and those cowering inside to get to the parapet first, those who won the race often won the battle though savage hand to hand fighting was common.

However the attack on Winchelsea actually took place, it was the English who gained the victory. The fighting continued from noon until sunset, but by then the French were no closer to getting into the town than they had been to start with. As dusk fell Vienne ordered his men to their ships and once again he put out to sea.

Either on the same day as the attack on Winchelsea or the next a smaller force of ships and men put into Hastings. Like Rye this was an important port in 1377. The French found the town empty and undefended, though the English chronicles fail to mention why the town had been abandoned. After breaking into the houses and failing to find anything very much worth stealing, the French set fire to the town. Once again a vast column of smoke went up into the sky as an English town was burned by the rampaging Franco-Castilian fleet.

Back at sea, Vienne and Tovar were still keen to find fresh prey. Their eyes went to that part of the Sussex coast where Brighton now stands.

During the 100 Years War the key military advantage that the English enjoyed was to have large numbers of competent archers armed with the longbow. The bow was not, in itself, particularly special although it was more powerful than comparable weapons used on the Continent. The key to the weapon's success came when large numbers of archers were massed together in specialist units on the battlefield, and each man was given unlimited numbers of arrows supplied by the king. Each man could fire upwards of six aimed shots each minute, so a thousand archers could deluge an enemy formation with a mass of arrows that became known as the "arrowstorm". At Brighton the English did not have enough trained archers to unleash an arrowstorm, and so they suffered accordingly.

30

Chapter 4
The Battle of Brighton

The Sussex coast where Brighton now stands was neither densely inhabited nor particularly prosperous in 1377. Brighton itself was then known as Brighthelmstone. It was an ancient place, being mentioned in the Domesday Book of 1087 and probably being some centuries old even then. It was a fishing village in 1377, but was larger than others for it had its own parish church and a regular market as well as a constable to enforce law and order. The town collectively paid a rent of 4,000 herrings annually.

The village of 1377 stood where The Lanes area is to be found today. The complex layout of The Lanes is usually held to be that of the original medieval village, though some parts may date to after the destruction of the village by fire in 1514. Brighton had no harbour in 1377, but the broad shingle beach with its shallow slope was ideal for fishing boats to be pulled up above high water mark for safety. The population would have numbered in the hundreds.

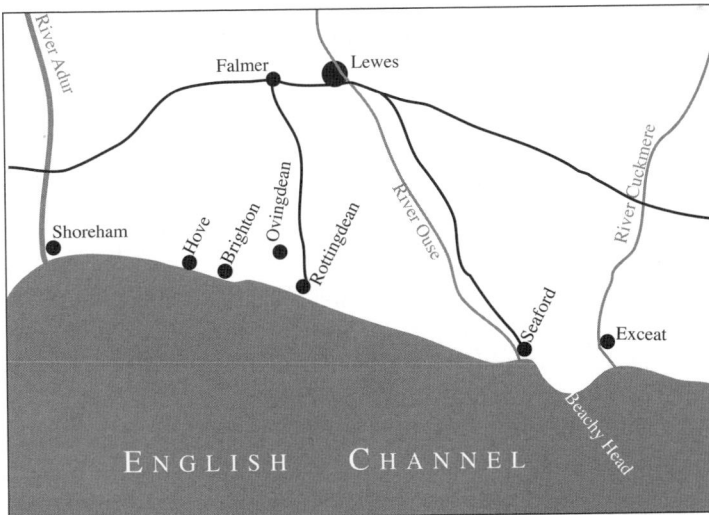

The coast around Brighton in 1377. The local militia were mustering in Lewes in anticipation of a French raid. The coastal villages of which Brighton was one of the largest had few defences.

31

To the west stood Hove, a smaller village of perhaps 50 inhabitants. This was another fishing village, with boats pulled up on to the beach. The few houses straggled inland along what is now Hove Street, though the parish church of St Andrew's stood in open fields some distance away to the northeast.

Further still to the west stood the small town of Shoreham, with its sheltered harbour at the mouth of the River Adur. Shoreham may have been small, but it was important. The River Adur gave a route through the towering heights of the South Downs to the lowlands beyond. Many ships called at Shoreham to shift cargoes into river barges that then nosed upstream to reach inland markets.

To the east of Brighton the coast rises to form cliffs. On top of the cliffs was open downland, though in a fold of the hills lay the village of Ovingdean with its 11th century church dedicated to St Wulfram of Sens. How many people lived here in 1377 is unknown, though it is unlikely to have been over 100.

The line of cliffs was broken slightly further east at Rottingdean. In 1377 this place was described as a town, though it had no defensive walls and seems to have been little more than a fairly large village. The rather inflated status accorded to the place might be due to the fact that the large parish church of St Margaret acted as a regional administrative centre for the Priory of Lewes, which owned much land in the area. There were a few houses by the sea, but most of the village lay inland around the church, which fronted on to a large, square village green.

East of Rottingdean were more towering chalk cliffs and beaches, but not much in the way of human settlement until the mouth of the River Ouse, which then lay at Seaford some distance to the east of his current outlet into the sea. Seaford, like Shoreham, was a reasonable sized town and a busy port.

Beyond the towering Seaford Head with its huge chalk cliffs that push out into the sea, lies the mouth of the Cuckmere River. A short distance up the Cuckmere was the village of Exceat, which had once been a naval base but was in 1377 rather in decline and had the status of a large village. East of the Cuckmere rose the towering heights of Beachy Head after which stretched almost desolate marshes and salt flats that reached to Hastings.

Only about five miles inland from the coast around Brighton stood the town of Lewes. This was a prosperous and busy place, the centre for the entire district both economically and administrively. The town stands on the River Ouse, commanding important routes that run both north-south and east-west. The town certainly existed before 1066 and may date back to Roman times, though the archaeological evidence is unclear.

In 1377 Lewes was the site of not only a prosperous town with stout town walls, but also a royal castle and one of the richest priories in the kingdom. It was a rich and important town, just the sort of place that Vienne and Tovar wanted to get their hands on. The question that they faced, was how to get there.

Five miles may not sound very far, and it is a distance that even a man encumbered with medieval armour could march in under two hours. However, for seaborne raiders entirely ignorant of where enemy armed forces might be lurking five miles is a long way. It is one thing to land at coastal towns such as Rye, but quite another to take the risk of marching inland. Nevertheless, Vienne and Tovar were here to do damage to England to aid their monarchs, and to gain loot for themselves. Lewes was worth the effort.

While we cannot know their plans in detail, the way the campaign developed

Brighton beach seen from the pier. The gently shelving beach gave easy access to the French raiders. The ships were anchored a short distance off shore and the men rowed to the beach in boats. In 1377 the village of Brighthelmstone occupied the area about 200 yards inland from the current seafront.

makes it clear that they intended to land on the coast somewhere south of Lewes and cause as much destruction and noise as possible while staying close to their ships. That should bring to the coast whatever armed forces were in the area. Vienne and Tovar would have their scouts out, so once they knew the scale of the opposition coming against them they could decide whether to stand and fight or to flee back to their ships. Even if they fled, they could claim a victory of sorts by having burned a number of coastal villages and gained plunder - even if it came in the form of barrels of dried fish. But if they won then the entire countryside for miles around would be open for them to pillage, and with luck they could take Lewes as well.

We don't know exactly where the French soldiers first came ashore. We do

The church at Rottingdean went up in flames as the French spread out inland. A small force of Englishmen put up minor resistance here, but were soon chased away by the much larger force of French invaders.

know that before long the first part of the raiders' plan was being successfully carried out. Brighton went up in flames as the invaders poured ashore. The inhabitants fled inland, though due to the speed with which the assault took place they do not seem to have had the chance to take anything much with them. Hove no doubt followed as the raiders sought to create columns of smoke to attract whatever forces were nearby.

Ovingdean certainly followed. To this day there are scorchmarks and discolouration caused by extreme heat on the walls of St Wulfran's Church. The marks are at their clearest on the south side of the nave. A south aisle that had been added in about 1250 was destroyed, presumably by fires begun by the French. To the east the pattern of destruction seems to have been more haphazard. Exceat was burned to the ground and utterly destroyed, so much so that it never recovered, while Seaford seems to have escaped fairly lightly. A manor house at Sutton by Seafield that was owned by Michael of Northburgh was also utterly destroyed. Northburgh later complained that he had lost property and livestock worth £100.

When the French reached Rottingdean there was a brief, but bloody skirmish. The only reference to this event is found in the Chronicle of Jean Froissart who mentions it in briefly when he says that the French took possession of Rottingdean "in spite of the English defenders, who did what they could".

This phase of the landing would have taken two or more hours as the French spread out to cause destruction, while ensuring that they were never far from each other so that they did not run the risk of falling prey to ambush by locals armed with axes or knives.

Scouts had meanwhile been sent riding inland to find out what the English were up to. They did not have long to wait.

In Lewes, Caroloco and the experienced knights with him will have seen the smoke columns going up as Brighton, Rottingdean and other places burned. Very soon the first fleeing refugees will have arrived to pour out the story of the landings and the attacks.

Driving off French raids was what the local militia were for, so it was time for action. We have no record of any discussions between Caroloco and the knights, but the conclusion was clear enough: they decided to march to the scene of action and attack the French. Over 500 armed men were gathered in Lewes, and while the reports from the refugees were far from clear they did not seem to indicate that the French massively outnumbered the English.

But that gave them a problem for between Lewes and the burning villages was the towering mass of the South Downs. For men in armour, and men on heavy war horses, it is not possible to simply march up the sort of steep escarpment as that presented by the north face of the South Downs at this point. One was to go southeast by way of Iford and Southease to Seaford, the other was to strike west to Falmer, then drive south through Ovingdean toward Rottingdean. The Prior of Lewes led his men by way of the more westerly route. It was now after noon, and the battle seems to have begun in the early evening.

As with all medieval battles it is not straightforward when dealing with the Battle of Brighton to establish exactly where the fighting took place, nor to trace the movements of the different units. Medieval chroniclers were far more concerned with relating the daring exploits of individual knights and nobles than

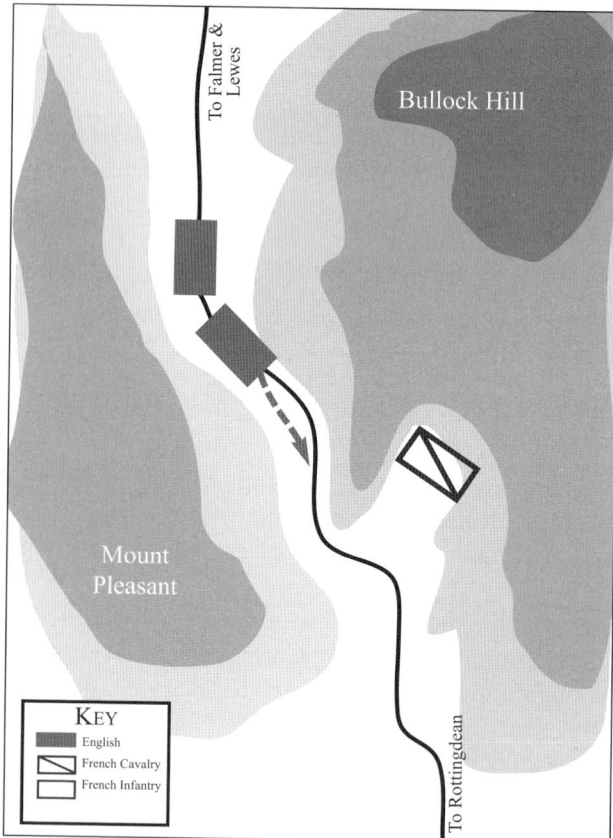

It was somewhere around 5pm that the Battle of Brighton properly got underway. French commander Jean de Vienne had been watching for an English relief force from a high vantage point, probably Bullock Hill northeast of Brighton. When he saw the English militia from Lewes approaching he withdrew his infantry to Rottingdean and hid his cavalry in a narrow valley where they would be out of sight of the advancing English.

with details of who stood where. For medieval audiences, the dash and glamour of chivalry came first, and the military detail came second.

This is particularly the case with this battle. Although three different chroniclers gave a detailed account of the action none of them agree with each other. Putting together a coherent account of where the battle took place and how it unfolded is a matter of judgement and opinion. What follows are my conclusions based on the available evidence and the lie of the land as it was in 1377. Others may well disagree with me, but I believe that this is how things happened.

The first problem is to decide where the battle took place. The chronicles of Jean Froissart (French) and Walsingham (English) are not much help here. Froissart says it was on the road towards Lewes, while Walsingham says it was near Rottingdean. Either could mean anything.

However, Jean Cabaret D'Orronville gives more detail. He says that "the Admiral [Vienne], who was no fool and had a strong suspicion that someone would arrive" and continues "They saw the English coming a long way off". Having tramped around the area it is clear that there are relatively few places where Vienne could have stood and seen "the English coming from a long way off". Most of the convenient high points have their view north along what is now the B2123 blocked by other hills. An exception is the western shoulder of Bullock Hill, which rises to over 600 feet and gives uninterrupted views north as far as Falmer, where the English would have turned off the main east-west road (now the A27) to go south to the burning villages.

D'Orronville continues that Vienne "had laid a great ambush of 300 cavalry, hand-picked men...and let the English get close, then they emerged from ambush and attacked them."

Although the description does not specify where the ambush that began the battle took place, it gives several strong clues. First, assuming that Vienne saw Caroloco coming from Bullock Hill while the English were at Falmer, he would have hurried back to his men (wherever they were at this point) and got them into a position that therefore must have been between Woodingdean and the sea. Second the English were clearly unaware of the French cavalry until the charge began, which means that Vienne managed to successfully hide 300 men mounted on horses in a place where they could not be seen by the advancing English column.

Third the hiding place was somewhere that allowed the French to launch a successful cavalry charge. That needs relatively flat, open land. Steep slopes, dense trees or hedges impede cavalry and seriously reduces the impact of a mounted charge.

There is no way of knowing precisely what the vegetation cover here was in 1377, but this was sheep country so there would not have been much in the way of forests or hedges. The dominant vegetation would have been grass, clipped short by grazing sheep. Most of this land is now covered by the houses of Woodingdean. Back in 1377 there was no such place. The entire area was built up in the 1920s on land that had belonged to Woodingdean Farm. Similarly the northern extension of Rottingdean did not exist in 1377. The road went through open countryside all the way from Falmer to Rottingdean Church. Along most of this length men marching south would have had a good, clear view of the land ahead meaning that an ambush would have been impossible.

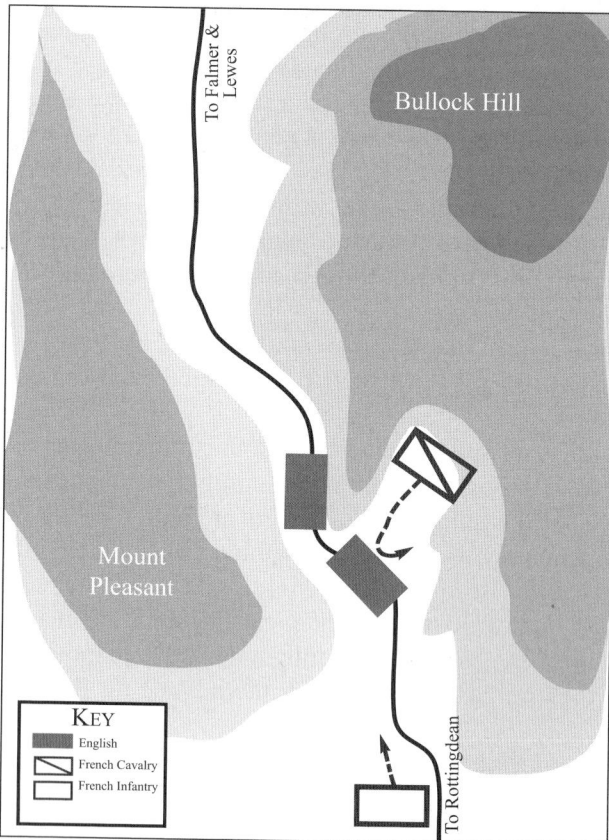

French commander Jean de Vienne sprang his trap as the English column of marching men passed by his hidden cavalry. Although the surprise seems to have been complete, the initial French charge was driven off as the English quickly got themselves into formation to face the onrush of armoured horsemen. Vienne may have responded by bringing his infantry forward from Rottingdean, though the contemporary sources are not clear on this point.

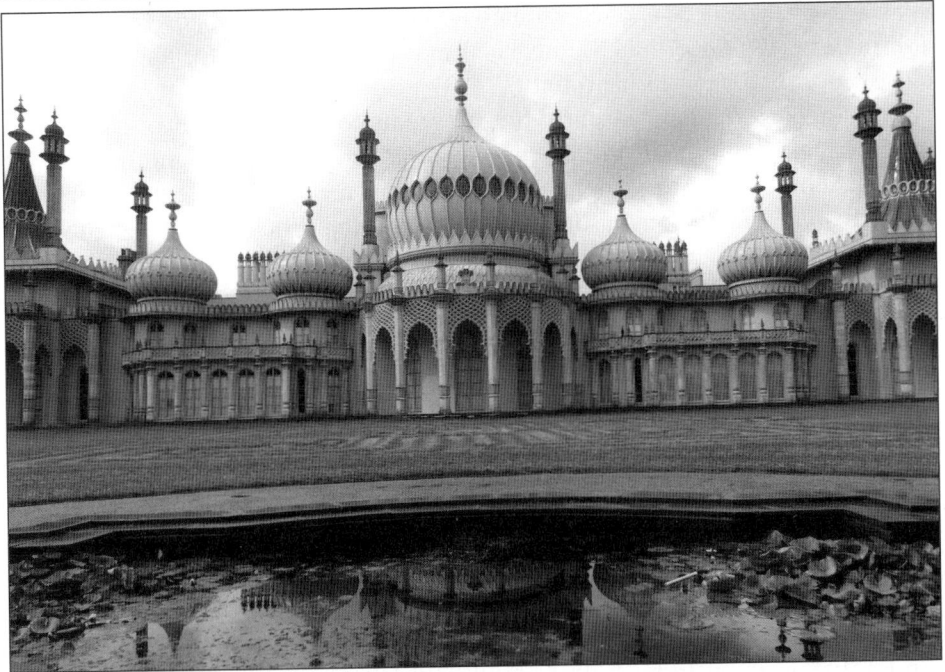

The magnificent Royal Pavilion is today one of the key attractions and landmarks of Brighton. In 1377 this site was open land across which the fugitives fleeing the battle fled, perhaps hoping to find sanctuary at the parish church which lies just to the west.

However, there is a spot where an ambush could have been sprung as D'Orronville describes. As the road twists through what is now called Happy Valley there is a side valley cutting away to the northeast. This valley is now partly built over by Cowley Drive and Ravenswood Drive of Woodingdean, but it is clear that horsemen standing in this valley could not be seen by men coming down the Falmer Road until the last minute. The floor of the valley is flat, level and smooth - ideal for a cavalry charge.

Not only that but on the west side of the Falmar Road are the steep slopes of Mount Pleasant. Anyone seeking to retreat back would find their escape route impeded by slopes too steep for organsied formations of men to keep their order. To Vienne this must have seemed like an ideal ambush site.

The picture given by D'Orronville is that the English were caught quite unawares by the charge and were routed in confusion. Froissart, however, supplies a different view. According to him The English "awaited the foe approaching in close order for a hand-to-hand fight."

Walsingham is more obscure, but he seems to agree with Froissart for he implies that at one point the English were advancing against the French. He recounts how an esquire "fought manfully against men of France, in so much that his belly (was) cut, he fought sore, his bowels remaining behind him a great space, and followed his enemies." Leaving aside the hideously painful death this man must have suffered, the only possible interpretation of the incident is that at some point the English were advancing and the French retreating.

All the sources agree that the English lost the battle. D'Orronville states baldly that the French "routed them and captured their leader." Froissart gives more detail "Finally the French conquered and dislodged the English; two hundred of them were killed and a large number of the more important men taken prisoner, rich men from the surrounding parts who had come there to win honour; the prior and the two knights were also taken."

Froissart gives the additional detail that Prior Caroloco was captured "in a square in front of a church".

The challenge is to try to make sense of all these clues. It seems that although the English were taken by surprise by the French cavalry charge, they were not

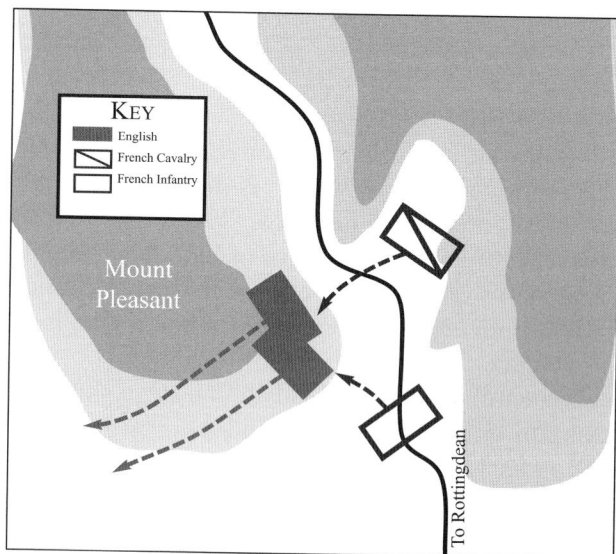

KEY
- English
- French Cavalry
- French Infantry

Mount Pleasant

To Rottingdean

The fighting that took place just outside Brighton, in an area now partly covered by suburbs, was over in less than an hour. The renewed assault by the French cavalry, probably backed by an infantry attack proved too much for the English militia who broke and fled southwest towards Brighton.

immediately defeated. It is likely that the English infantry, for most militia were infantry at this date, managed to form themselves into a dense phalanx and present their shields and spears to the enemy before the cavalry charged home.

No doubt there were casualties on both sides, but this first charge seems to have been unsuccessful. Standard tactics for the time would have seen the French cavalry pull back and trot away to reform ready for another charge. Perhaps it was at this point that the hapless squire "followed his enemies".

None of the accounts of the battle mention the French infantry, but they could not have been very far away. D'Orronville states that Vienne had 2,000 men ashore in all. With 400 mounted that leaves 1,600 on foot. Vienne may have launched a second cavalry charge, or he may have brought up his infantry. It would have depended on how shaken he thought the English were by the first assault. If they looked like a second attack would break them, Vienne would have been sensible to hurl his horsemen forward, otherwise he would await his infantry.

It is possible to read too much into passing remarks, but Froissart does seem to imply that the fighting lasted for some time, so perhaps the French infantry did play a role.

Whatever the detail of the fight, the English clearly eventually gave way and fled. Froissart's comment that Prior Caroloco was captured by a church implies that they fled to a village. The nearest village, and the one that lay in the opposite direction to that from which the French had attacked was Ovingdean. However,

The final stages of the pursuit seem to have been played out around St Nicholas's Church, the old medieval parish church of Brighton. It was here that the English commander was captured.

41

there is no evidence that there was ever a "square" in front of the church such as is described.

Following the most likely route taken by English fugitives fleeing the battlefield, the next settlement was Brighton. The buildings around St Nicholas' Church in Brighton were destroyed by the fire of 1514 and have been radically redeveloped several times since. Whether or not there was a "square" in front of this church it is impossible to know. Since there was not one at Ovingdean, and Brighton is the next place the fugitives would have reached it is reasonable to assume that this is where Caroloco was captured. This means that the final stages of the battle were played around where the famous Brighton Pavilion now stands. The area has been densely built over, so nothing much remains as it would have been in 1377, other than the church.

At any rate the battle must have seemed to be over when Prior Caroloco was captured. The surviving men of the English army were in flight. Froissart says that 200 of them were killed, Walsingham says 100 died. Whatever the truth, the

Rottingdean High Street. It seems to have been here that the English under the Earl of Salisbury captured the French wounded who had been left behind by Vienne as he fled back to his ships.

army was now leaderless and in flight. It had ceased to exist as a fighting force. Vienne and Tovar had achieved their aim. They had crushed the local defence force and could now look forward to the opportunity of spreading out over the countryside to plunder and loot as they liked. They could even hope to capture the town of Lewes, or at least extort a huge sum of money as they had done on the Isle of Wight.

It was not to be. While all this had been going on around Brighton, the Earl of Salisbury and his army had been continuing along the road to Lewes from the west. Whether they were told by locals that Caroloco had marched south to fight the French, or if they too saw the columns of smoke from the burning villages and drew their own conclusions we do not know. We do know that Salisbury marched toward the scene of conflict.

It must be that Vienne's scouts saw the new and larger English army approaching, for the French retreat back to their ships was hurried and disorganised. They left behind them several of their wounded men, who were swiftly captured by Salisbury and his advancing men.

Froissart records what sounds like an excuse offered by Salisbury, or perhaps by his men, when he writes "The Earl of Salisbury was unable to get there in time, because of the rough roads and difficult going."

Whatever the case, Salisbury got there too late to save Caroloco and his men, but did drive off the raiders and so stopped them from rampaging destructively through Sussex.

As was the custom, Salisbury questioned his prisoners about the enemy leaders and their intentions. One of the prisoners told him something that was to have an impact on England's internal politics. "We would never have dared to land," the man said, "if the Duke of Lancaster had been made king." John of Gaunt, Duke of Lancaster, and his supporters used this remark to demand an increased role for him in the government, sparking of a renewed round of political turmoil at the top of English government.

It should be said that some historians draw different conclusions from the sparse account in the chronicles. They believe that the ambush and fighting all took place on the village green at Rottingdean. In their favour it can be said that the village green is square in shape and abuts the church. However, it is a small space for 3,000 men to fight a battle, and street fighting is not suitable for a cavalry action for which reasons I consider this view to be mistaken.

Chapter 5
Aftermath

The immediate aftermath of the battle was that, once again, the French put to sea with their Castilian allies and went off in search of new places to attack and plunder. The sources are divided as to where they went next. A French chronicle says that they went first to "Pesk", but there is no such place on the south coast of England, and then to Plymouth where they burnt and pillaged some farms before sailing away again and heading to Dover.

The English sources make no mention of an attack on lands near Plymouth or Pesk (wherever that was) but do mention a descent upon Dover in the first week of September. Given the distance to Plymouth and back it seems unlikely that the entire Franco-Castilian fleet went all the way to Devon, then came all the way back again. Most likely it was a detachment of just a few ships that went west, presumably inflicting so little damage that the English did not think it worthy of mention.

All sources agree that the next important action after the fight at Brighton took place at Dover. The port of Dover is dominated by the mighty castle, founded in 1066 but massively enlarged and strengthened in the 12th and 13th centuries. By the time the raiders arrived off Dover the Earl of Cambridge was back in residence. He had by now cemented his position on the Council of Nobles that was advising the child-king Richard II and had outmanoeuvred his brother John of Gaunt who had no official position in the government. Cambridge was, therefore, free of domestic disputes to pay attention to what should have been his main task all along - defending England from the French.

Cambridge had brought to Dover a large army, which he paraded on the shoreline, daring the enemy to land and give battle. For seven days the Franco-Castilian fleet lay anchored off Dover while the two forces eyed each other warily. On the eighth day a storm blew up and Tovar ordered his ships to lift their anchors and put out to sea to get away from a potentially dangerous coastline.

Once at sea, Vienne and Tovar decided that they had achieved enough. For two months they had cruised unopposed up and down the English Channel. They had sent two English towns and dozens of villages up in flames, and stolen or extracted by threats a huge amount of booty. It was time to go home. They made for Harfleur where the men were paid off and the French ships laid up for the winter, while the Castilian fleet returned to Spain.

The architect of French strategy, Bertrand du Guesclin, did not have long to live. In 1380 he was leading yet another campaign against the English in southern France when he fell ill while laying siege to the castle of Chateauneuf-de-Randon. He retired to his tent, but his unidentified sickness grew rapidly worse and within a couple of days he was dead. He was accorded the rare honour of being buried in the royal crypt at Saint-Denis, the royal abbey near Paris.

The two successful commanders on the ground enjoyed rather better future careers. Jean de Vienne used his successful campaign of 1377 to extract more men and money out of Charles V. However, his plans to attack England were thwarted by Charles's insistence that he use his resources against Flanders. It was not until 1385 that Vienne gathered together a fleet of 185 ships to invade England. The large French force sailed to Scotland to rendezvous with a Scottish army for a joint invasion of northern England. Unfortunately, Vienne quarrelled with the Earl of Douglas, his Scottish partner, over how to lay siege to Roxburgh Castle. When it transpired that Vienne had been correct in his analysis of the English defences, Douglas stormed off and withdrew the Scottish army leaving Vienne stranded. Vienne marched back to his ships and went home in a fury.

Worse was to follow for Vienne. The new French king Charles VI went mad in 1392 and the French government was paralysed by bickering and disputes between the leading nobles over who should be regent, who should sit on the Council and who should have lucrative posts. In the squabbling the importance of funding a navy was forgotten and Vienne found himself without money to pay his men or maintain his ships. In disgust he went on crusade to fight the Moslem forces invading southeastern Europe. He achieved several small victories before being killed in the disastrous Battle of Nicopolis in September 1396, which saw the Ottoman Turks virtually annihilate a joint army of Bulgars and Crusaders.

Fernando Sánchez de Tovar brought his Castilian fleet back to English waters in 1380. His daring plan was to sail up the Thames to attack London. He captured Gravesend and burned the town to the ground, then patrolled the Thames Estuary, capturing dozens of richly laden merchant ships as they entered what they erroneously thought would be safe waters. The defences of London proved too much for him, but he did manage to disrupt English trade for months for even after he had left the Thames merchants did not dare put to sea in case he was lurking just over the horizon.

The following year Tovar was created Lord of Belves by King John I of Castile, the son and successor of Henry of Trastamara. He then won a crushing victory over the Portuguese navy at the Battle of Saltes Island. In 1383 King Ferdinand of Portugal died without an heir. His illegitimate son John of Avis was proclaimed king, but John of Castile remembered he had a slight claim to the crown and launched an invasion. Tova was sent to blockade the Portuguese coast. He died at some point in the summer of 1384 at sea off Lisbon.

The Earl of Cambridge retained his position at the heart of English government and society for the rest of his life. He was never again given a military command, but instead remained in England. He acted as regent for Richard II when he went abroad on three occasions. However, when his two nephews Richard II and

The death of Bertrand du Guesclin from a contemporary manuscript. The loss of this talented commander brought to an end the French strategic offences and before long England and France patched up a peace treaty that brought the long years of warfare to an end, albeit only a temporary one.

Henry, son of John of Gaunt, came to blows in 1399 he chose to back Henry and was instrumental in making him king as Henry IV. Cambridge died at his manor of Abbots Langley on 1 August 1402 and was buried in the priory there. His tomb was destroyed during the Reformation.

Sir Thomas Arundel who had driven the French away from Southampton was rewarded by being appointed Lord Marshal of England and given permission to turn his manor house at Betchworth in Surrey into a castle. However, he came to a violent end. In 1379 he was given command of a small fleet taking supplies from Southampton to the Duke of Brittany to aid him in his war against France.

Contrary winds kept the fleet in port and some of Arundel's men went ashore. Exactly what happened is unclear, but the men appear to have got drunk and broke into a small convent. Certainly they stole property from the convent and according to one source they raped some of the nuns. Eager to save his men from the vengeance of the townsfolk of Southampton, which may have delayed his departure even further, Arundel hurriedly put to sea and was caught in a gale which blew him to the south coast of Ireland. With the threat of imminent wreck on the rocky shore, Arundel killed the men who had raped the nuns and had their bodies thrown into the sea. At this point a huge wave crashed over the decks of his ship and Arundel was swept overboard. The storm abated shortly after and his men were able to retrieve his body, which they took back to England for burial in Lewes Priory, now a ruin.

Abbot Harno de Offynton returned to his work as Abbot of Battle Abbey, a position he held until his death in 1383.

Sir Hugh Tyrrel who defended Carisbrooke Castle remained governor there until 1382 and subsequently held a series of relatively minor government positions. He died in 1408.

John de Caroloco, Prior of Lewes, was held a prisoner in France for almost a year. He was released only when Vienne received a ransom payment of 7,000 gold nobles, each noble being worth 80 pennies. This was a standard ransom for a nobleman captured in medieval times as it was the equivalent to two years income for the priory. He returned to Lewes and remained Prior to his death in 1396.

The ransom for Sir Thomas Cheyne was set at 300 marks, the precise sum that was his share in ransom money gained in earlier fighting in France. Cheyne did not have the money as it was still owed to him by his then commander in chief, the Black Prince who had died in 1376. He was released at Easter 1379 after

Vienne got his money, though we don't know who paid it. Cheyne died at home in March 1381.

Sir John Falvesley was released, though there is no record of any ransom being paid, and in 1382 he married Elizabeth Say. He was later in service with the Earls of Arundel and died in 1392.

John Brocas died in French captivity on 26 September 1377, probably due a wound sustained in the battle. He left no children and his young widow, Sybil, was soon remarried to another knight Sir John Uvedale of Titsey Park in Surrey.

Thomas Wilford was released in the spring of 1378. His date of death is unknown but he appears intermittently in local records until 1387.

The Earl of Salisbury, who failed to get to the battle in time to take part, joined Richard II on a minor border war with Scotland in 1385 but otherwise led a quiet life after 1377. He died in 1397.

Peace was declared between England and France in 1389. Neither the economic rivalries nor the dynastic disputes that had begun the war had been solved, it was more that both kingdoms were exhausted by war and riven by internal disputes and so in no condition to continue fighting. The war broke out again, however, and raged on until 1453.

ALSO AVAILABLE IN THIS SERIES

The Battle of Wimbledon 568
The Battle of Crug Mawr 1136
The Battle of Lincoln 1141
The Battle of Lewes 1264
The Battle of Chesterfield 1266
The Battle of Bannockburn 1314
The Battle of Brighton 1377
The Battle of Northampton 1460
The Battle of Towton 1461
The Battle of Losecoat Field 1470
The Battle of Bosworth 1485
The Sieges of Newark 1643-46
The Siege of Leicester 1645